# games people play!

# China

## Kim Dramer

**CHILDREN'S PRESS®**
A Division of Grolier Publishing
New York • London • Hong Kong • Sydney
Danbury, Connecticut

**Author's Dedication**

*For my Chinese family.*


**Design Staff**

*Design and Electronic Composition:*
  TJS Design

*Maps:* TJS Design

*Cover Art and Icons:* Susan Kwas

**Library of Congress Cataloging-in-Publication Data**

Dramer, Kim.
China/Kim Dramer.
p.  cm. — (Games people play)
Includes bibliographical references and index.
Summary: Discusses the ways that Chinese children have amused
themselves from ancient times to the present, with such games,
toys and sports as Chinese checkers, tangrams, paper folding,
stilts, kites, ping pong, and martial arts.
ISBN 0-516-20308-8
1. Recreation—China—History—Juvenile literature.
[1. Recreation—China  2. Games—China.  3. Sports—China.]
I. Title.  II. Series.

GV121.D73  1997                    96-40972
790'.0951—dc20                        CIP
                                      AC

# Table of  ontents

# Introduction

# A Land Of Traditions

In traditional China, games and toys were reserved for babies and young children. Once they reached school age, Chinese children were encouraged to focus only on their studies.

Chinese parents love and treasure their children.

Archaeologists have discovered toys and games more than six thousand years old in Chinese sites. China's ancient culture has profoundly influenced the games American children play today. Kites, tops, yo-yos, POGS, and puzzles all have their roots in China.

A Chinese saying states: "Children are more valuable than jade." The saying has never been more true than in modern China. The government currently enforces a policy restricting families from having more than one child. This rule is intended to help stop China's population from growing out of control. Because families have just one child, parents and grandparents tend to lavish love and gifts on the single child in the house. Many Chinese refer to these children as "little emperors and empresses."

Being the family's only child means a great deal of pressure to succeed in school. Parents in today's China often give gifts, such as music, calligraphy, and painting lessons to help children succeed in their studies. But after lessons are done, Chinese children love to play games and sports.

Over the centuries, Chinese toys have been made of simple paper as well as costly silk. They have been either plain or lavishly decorated. Chinese games have ranged from the simple to the complex. This book will explore some

Chinese games from their beginnings to the present. You will see how these games have changed over time to reflect new beliefs, inventions, ideas, or attitudes.

The population of China is so enormous that today, one out of every six children in the world is Chinese. The games that today's Chinese children play may be ancient or new. The toys may be made by traditional Chinese craftsmen or imported from the West. Inventiveness, paired with respect for tradition, remain the basis for China's culture and its games.

In this book, you will learn all about China's traditions and culture and how they are expressed in sports and games. For instance, you'll find that the dragon is an important symbol in Chinese culture, and it can be found in many activities (such as dragon boat racing, bottom). Chinese checkers (below, left) is a popular game with a long history — but have you heard of Chinese chess? You'll also discover that in China, people have fun doing the same things you do, such as collecting stamps (below), but they also enjoy many activities you don't, such as walking on stilts (left).

# **M**ajor Chinese Dynasties

Most of Chinese history can be divided into dynasties, during which the country was ruled by emperors called "Sons of Heaven." Throughout his reign, the emperor asked blessings of heaven to ensure a good harvest, peace, and prosperity throughout the Empire. When emperors acted unrighteously, they were removed from power by his subjects. This timeline shows some of the major dynasties in Chinese history.

   The last dynasty ended in 1912, when a revolution produced a republic as the Chinese government. After a civil war in the 1940s, the Communist People's Republic of China was founded and rules mainland China today.

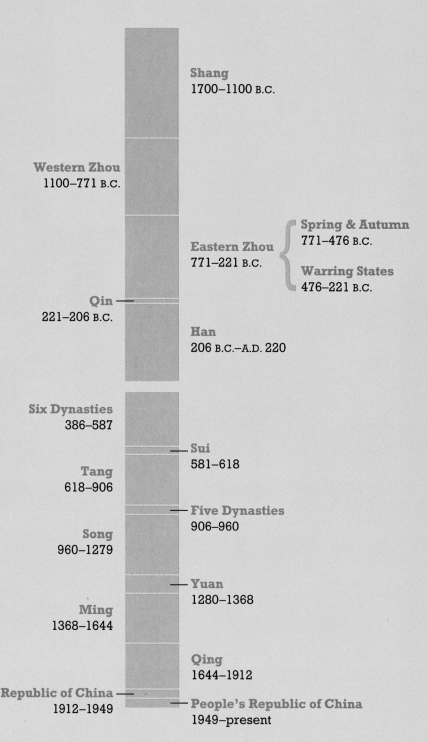

**Shang**
1700–1100 B.C.

**Western Zhou**
1100–771 B.C.

**Eastern Zhou**
771–221 B.C.

**Spring & Autumn**
771–476 B.C.

**Warring States**
476–221 B.C.

**Qin**
221–206 B.C.

**Han**
206 B.C.–A.D. 220

**Six Dynasties**
386–587

**Sui**
581–618

**Tang**
618–906

**Five Dynasties**
906–960

**Song**
960–1279

**Yuan**
1280–1368

**Ming**
1368–1644

**Qing**
1644–1912

**Republic of China**
1912–1949

**People's Republic of China**
1949–present

People's Republic of China is the official name of China. With an
area of 3.7 million square miles (9.6 square kilometers), China
is only slightly larger than the United States; however China's
population of one billion is about four times larger than that of
the United States. China's capital city is Beijing, and its largest
city is Shanghai, with a population of more than 7.5 million.

# Chapter One
# Traditional Festivals and Games of China

Chinese society is agrarian, which means that it follows a farming calendar. The rhythm of daily life and festivals is set by the rhythm of nature and the harvesting of crops. Many traditional Chinese festivals and their amusements are linked to the agrarian calendar.

As the **Lunar New Year** starts, the dragons sleep. According to Chinese legend, a dragon is a creature that brings rain as it soars through the air and dives into the rivers below. Dragons must awaken after the winter season of drought to bring rains to drench the parched earth so that wheat, millet, and rice may be planted once again. Crackling explosions of fireworks accompany huge dragons made of bamboo, cloth, and paper as they are paraded through fields and streets during the Lunar New Year celebration. Banging drums and clashing cymbals add to the excitement of the New Year procession.

In an agrarian society, most people are involved with working on the land and producing food.

Chinese New Year traditions include spectacular fireworks displays.

The bamboo dragon spits lightning of fireworks. Children set off colored rockets that light up the New Year sky. The Chinese call fireworks *yan huo*, or "smoke and fire." Gunpowder, a Chinese invention, is the main ingredient in fireworks.

Chinese children explode their fireworks to awaken the dragons at the Lunar New Year and to chase off all the evil spirits that might plague their households. They spend the day with their families and receive red envelopes of lucky money. Chinese children make sure that the doors on their house are framed with spring couplets. These are special poems written on red paper expressing hopes for happiness during the coming year.

The Chinese conclude the Lunar New Year celebrations after fifteen days with the **Lantern Festival**. On this day, children carry colorful lanterns of fantastic shapes. In the evening, the children light their lanterns and go with their families and friends to lantern fairs. Here they compare their lanterns with those of other children and launch kites in the form of lanterns. The night sky fills with floating lights, slowly rising. The kites, rising higher and higher, symbolize the families' hopes for their children.

**Riddle-guessing contests** are the traditional game during the Lantern Festival. Most of the riddles told at the Lantern Festival test a child's ability to write Chinese characters.

Placing couplets on the sides of the family's front door is another Chinese New Year tradition.

Placing flowers at a family grave during the Festival of Spring Brightness

The **Festival of Spring Brightness** is also known as the **Tomb Sweeping Festival**. The family spends this holiday at the graves of their ancestors. They tidy the graves and make offerings of food and wine. Kite flying is a traditional amusement during this festival. Chinese children launch kites and let them fly away. This custom is possibly tied to ancient religious rituals. In this way, the ancient Chinese explained, diseases and calamities might also be carried off.

Crafting a dragon boat

In the summer, the **Dragon Boat Festival** features boat races. Teams compete in elaborately decorated dragon-shaped boats. The festival commemorates the sacrifice of the ancient patriot-poet, Qu Yuan, of the Warring States Period (476–221 B.C.), who hurled himself into the Miluo River out of despair over the future of his country.

During this festival, kites are used to drive away evil and send up prayers for blessings. For the same purpose, branches of fragrant herbs are hung on houses and children receive fragrant sachets to hang around their necks.

Competitors race their boats during the Dragon Boat Festival. The drummer beats time for the rowers.

The **Mid-Autumn Festival** is a time when Chinese practice the ancient custom of story-telling beneath the full autumn moon. On the day of this festival, the moon is at its roundest and brightest. Children gather with their families to gaze at the moon and hear ancient tales from their grandparents. While listening to stories, Chinese children eat round mooncakes symbolic of the completeness of a family reunited for the holidays.

# Chapter Two
# Games of Intellect

Archaeologists have found examples of counters, dice, and marked stones in ancient sites throughout China. Archaeologists believe that these items were used in games. But these were not games of chance, some were attempts to predict the future.

In early China, a man played dice not with another man, but with the gods. Today, such games of wits remain one of the most popular forms of amusement in China.

In the Spring and Autumn Period of China (771–221 B.C.), Confucius recommended the ancient game of **weiqi** as being good for the mind. In this game, each of two players has approximately two hundred pieces, called *zi*, arranged on a large board divided into squares. Originally, smooth black and white river pebbles served as the pieces. The object of the game is to surround and invade enemy forces, thus eliminating them from play. Most Americans know this game by its Japanese name — *go*. The Chinese term for the game is literally translated as "surround chess."

Playing *weiqi* ("surround chess"), a game known in Japan as *go*.

The Chinese chess board is similar to the checkers board used in the West.

In the game of **Chinese chess**, two armies fight against each other as generals protect their fortresses. Elephants, horsemen, cavalry, cannon, war chariots, and infantry march across a board marked out in 64 squares. As in Western chess, the object of the game is to capture the opposing side's king.

The chessmen in Chinese chess are not the elaborately carved figures found in Western chess. Each piece is round, with the character marked in either red or black. Unlike Western chess, the pieces are placed on the intersections of the lines on the board. Across the center of the board stretches "the river," a space that the pieces cannot cross.

Chinese children enjoy a version of checkers played by three players. The three sides in **Chinese checkers** compete on a wooden board marked out by two overlapping triangles that form a star. The goal of each of the three players is to be the first to move all of his or her pieces to the opposite side of the board. A player can jump over his own or another player's pieces in the race. The Chinese call this game *tiaoqi*, or "jumping chess."

**Majiang** is a complex and sophisticated game that has gained great popularity in the United States (where it is called "mah-jongg"). In majiang, four players compete to build or break a wall. Some experts believe that the game refers to the Great Wall of China, one of the wonders of the world. The Great Wall is so large

Majiang players

that it is the only human construction on Earth that was visible to astronauts when they walked on the moon.

Majiang pieces (or tiles) resemble both dominoes and playing cards. Chinese craftsmen have created superb examples of majiang pieces in bone, ivory, bamboo, mother-of-pearl, and jade. The Chinese term for this game means "sparrow." Perhaps the clicking sound of majiang pieces was thought to resemble the chirping of tiny sparrows.

Some historians believe that many Chinese puzzles originated as exercises in concentration or as part of the religious disciplines of meditation. Tangrams and the Nine Connected Rings Puzzle are mentioned in ancient Chinese documents that are hundreds of years old.

The **tangram** is a square divided into seven pieces. It is similar to a Western jigsaw puzzle, but it differs from the jigsaw in always having only seven pieces. These pieces can be arranged to form the outlines of countless different objects and shapes. Pictures of people, animals, plants, and objects can be made, using only the seven pieces.

The tangram is sometimes called the "wisdom puzzle" in English. The Chinese term is *qi qiao ban*, or "seven-board of cunning." The tangram was invented during the Northern and Southern Dynasties over 1,500 years ago. It has remained popular

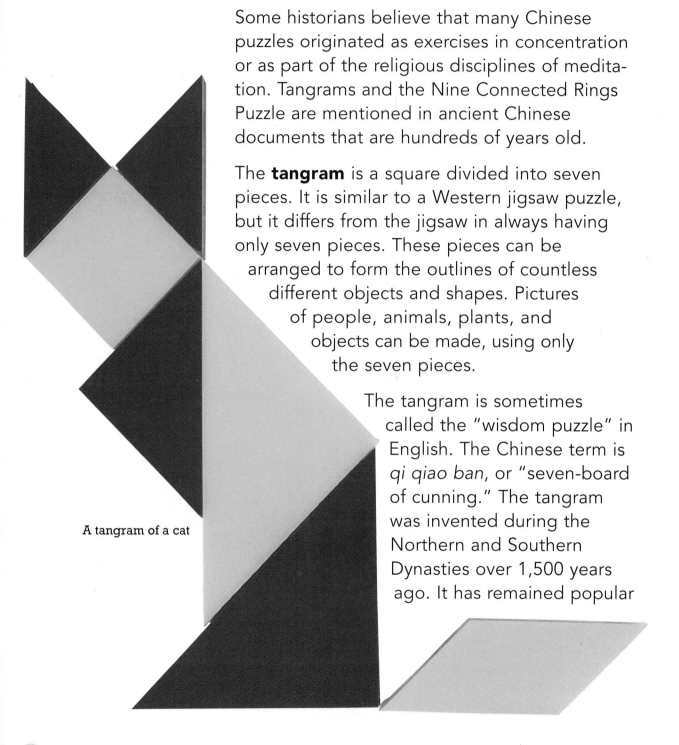

A tangram of a cat

Tangrams can provide hours of fun.

in China to this day and is used in schools to teach trigonometry and even geography.

The **Nine Connected Rings** puzzle consists of nine rings mysteriously attached to a long stick fitted into a carved handle. The object is to remove all nine rings from the loop — a process involving 511 separate movements of the puzzle. The complexity of the operation led to one Chinese name for the puzzle: "Detain your Guest."

The puzzle also has practical applications. The Chinese used the complex manipulations to devise efficient locks for strongboxes. To open the lock, one needed to make a number of complicated moves in the correct order.

In the 1800s, tangrams were one element of a box of Chinese games produced for export to the West. Tangrams became popular in North America and in Europe. Napoleon is reputed to have whiled away time during his exile on St. Helena with the intricacies of the tangram.

# How Do I Play?

**1.** Use a square piece of cardboard that is about 5"x5" (12.7 x 12.7 cm) or larger.

**2.** Following the diagram, cut the cardboard into these seven shapes.

**3.** Rearrange the seven shapes to make a sailboat (left) and a house (right).

**4.** Now, use your imagination to make some of the objects shown below and make up your own tangrams!

Children in China (and around the world) play with Pick Up Sticks.

Another game of skill enjoyed by Chinese children is the game of **Pick Up Sticks**. The game is played with a group of about 30 delicately carved ivory or bamboo sticks. The ends of the pieces are often carved in the shapes of crosses, lances, or swords.

The pieces are dropped at random onto the table. Each player, in turn, tries to lift up a single piece without touching or moving any of the others. Each piece has an allotted value that is counted up at the end to determine the winner of the game.

Pick Up Sticks may have evolved from fortune-telling practices. Today, many Chinese still visit fortune tellers who read their future by means of a dried yarrow stalk or small wooden sticks similar to Pick Up Sticks. The practice of casting lots is sometimes referred to by the alternate name "Jackstraws." Perhaps the game has its origins in the practice of predicting the success of a hunt by allowing a quiver of arrows to spill on the ground and interpreting the patterns of the sticks. Spilled objects might explain the term "Spillikins" — the British term for Pick Up Sticks.

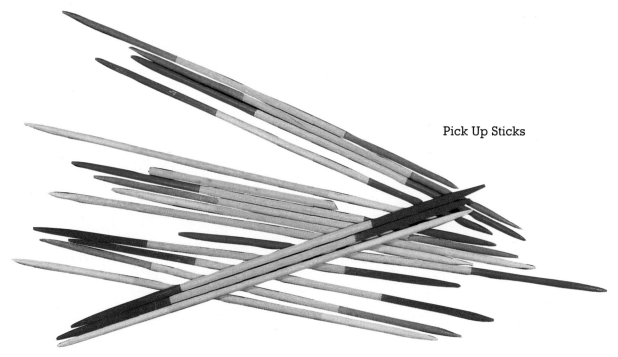

Pick Up Sticks

# Chapter Three

# Games and Amusements for Children

Reading and writing are very important skills to the Chinese. The tools of writing — such as paper, silk and bamboo — are found in all aspects of Chinese culture, including its toys, games, and hobbies. Many of these games have found their way into American culture as well.

Many Chinese games and amusements are made from the country's natural resources, such as its bamboo, hardwood, and silk. Also, silkworms feed on mulberry leaves and spin cocoons that are later turned into silk thread.

Ancient Chinese documents were written on both silk and wood. Strips of bamboo fastened together with string or on scrolls of silk were cumbersome and the silk was too expensive. Chinese culture responded with the invention of paper during the Han Dynasty (206 B.C.–A.D. 220).

With the invention of paper, many people learned to read and write. Eventually China invented the first postal system in the world.

Today, **stamp collecting** is the number-one hobby in China for adults and children alike. Tiny paper postage stamps from around the world are avidly collected by many Chinese.

Some Chinese postage stamps feature traditional arts, festivals, history and literature as their subjects. As ambassadors of China's culture around the world, these stamps signal the pride of the Chinese in their traditional culture.

Once paper became inexpensive and easily available, a vast array of toys were manufactured from brightly colored paper. Paper was cut or folded into a variety of shapes for games and amusements.

One example of a folded paper toy is **POGS**, a popular game recently introduced in the United States. In the Chinese version of POGS, paper is folded into triangles or *sanjiao*. POGS can be played with several players. Each player has a collection of POGS. The object is to "whip" over the other players' POG with one's own piece.

Chinese papercraft can produce delicate and beautiful objects, as well as POGS or airplanes (right), which kids love to throw through the air.

At traditional festival celebrations across China, vendors of folkcrafts sell brightly colored animals made of folded paper. Americans often refer to these toys by the Japanese term origami.

Folded flowers, pinwheels, and animals are enjoyed by Chinese children. In public markets, vendors place toys on long bamboo poles and walk among crowds selling their wares.

Paper-cut materials are inexpensive and easily available. Chinese craftspeople using scissors, gouges, and punches, are famous for their skill and creativity in paper-cuts. Paper-cuts often express the hopes and wishes of China's people. Chinese characters with messages of luck, longevity, and happiness may appear in the paper-cut design. Other paper-cuts include designs with symbolic meanings for longevity (peach, pine, and crane), fertility (pomegranate), or strength (lion, rooster and tiger). Other designs relate to specific words. Fish (*yu* in Chinese) symbolize abundance since both "fish" and "plenty" sound the same in Chinese.

It takes a lot of careful, patient work to produce paper-cut figures such as this crane.

Silk thread is used to tie intricate knots for decorating furniture, clothing, and household implements. These knots are known as **macramé**. The Chinese have manufactured silk since at least 3,000 B.C. and have perfected the art of macramé over the centuries. Chinese macramé involves tying, tightening, and then adding finishing touches to the knots. Macramé knots are especially popular as good luck charms worn around the neck and exchanged by school friends. Today, many American schoolchildren exchange "friendship bracelets" of macramé.

**Spinning toys** are other amusements that date back to Chinese prehistory and remain popular with Chinese children today. Tops are made of bamboo or hardwood and are spun with a cord twined around the spindle and pulled sharply. In southern China, iron spindles are driven through lotus seedpods, or conch shells are ground down to form tops. Tiny balancing tops are also manufactured from acorns.

Some Chinese children play a game in which they turn themselves into spinning toys. A circle is drawn on the ground and the child folds his or her arms across the chest. Next, using one hand to hold an ear, the child spins around and around trying not to step outside the circle.

Another form of Chinese spinning toy has gained great popularity in America — two disks of wood that travel up and down a string. In 1932, the Louis toy company in the United States copyrighted the name "yo-yo." The toy company proceeded to sell 100 million of these spinning toys invented by the Chinese.

Chinese spinning tops come in many sizes — large (below) and small (above). The man above is spinning a top called a diabolo.

Wood is used to manufacture another traditional form of Chinese recreation. Two wooden poles with footstops are used by the Chinese in **stiltwalking**. This form of amusement has been a tradition since the Zhou Dynasty (1100–221 B.C.). Today, dancers on stilts perform to traditional Chinese folktunes or operas and are a popular form of entertainment during parades.

Chinese acrobats entertain on stilts.

A soaring dragonfly, a chirping cricket, a buzzing cicada, and a hopping grasshopper could all be pets for Chinese children. These insects are kept in cages made of bamboo or split straws, or in a hollow, decorated gourd. Chinese have also used these pets for a variety of games since ancient times.

In China, cricket fights are a popular amusement.

During the Tang Dynasty (A.D. 618–906), **crickets** were trained to sing and fight. At the capital in Chang An (today's Xian), wealthy people staged matches pitting one fighting cricket against another. Spectators placed large bets on the cricket they believed would win the fight.

Today, many Chinese children keep a cricket as a pet during the summer months. The evening chirping of the cricket is the lullaby to which they fall asleep during the warm summer nights.

## cicada

an insect with a wide body and large, transparent wings that make a loud, buzzing noise

Each summer in China, the shrill song of **cicadas** fills the air at sunset. The sound of the cicada is produced by vibrating membranes near the abdomen of the male cicada. The cicada has two pairs of membranous wings. It lives high up in the trees. To capture a cicada, Chinese children use something resembling a fishing rod — a long bamboo pole with home-made glue on one end. Once the cicada is stuck on the pole, the child flies his or her insect "airplane" on the pole. Eventually the cicada is released.

Another insect Chinese children seek during the warm weather is the **dragonfly**. Dragonflies can be captured and placed on a leash — a thread tied around the insect's tiny waist. By pulling on the thread, a child can steer the insect through the sky like a kite and then release it.

A bamboo spinning toy that flies through the air is also called a dragonfly by the Chinese. A strip of bamboo is fitted with a central stick inserted in the middle to form a T-shape. The bamboo dragonfly is launched into the air by placing the stick between the palms and rubbing them quickly in opposite directions.

**Grasshoppers** are hunted in the long summer grass and also kept as pets by Chinese children.

Grasshoppers (bottom) are often kept as pets in cages (top). Some Chinese children tie strings around their bug pets as leashes.

Contests are held to see whose insect can jump the highest. Or, grasshoppers might be fashioned from palm leaves. The leaf is split and the fronds wrapped around the stem to form a realistic-looking animal.

# Chapter Four
# Kites

As winds sweep across China, lush stands of bamboos bend their branches. In groves of mulberry trees, silkworms spin their cocoons. Early in their history, the Chinese combined native bamboo and silk to make kites.

For the Chinese, kites were tools before they were toys. The first Chinese kites were related to religion, a sort of ancient mode of communication with the spirits on high. Silk kites carrying messages hoping for rain or good crops were flown and released. The ancient Chinese believed that their messages would eventually reach the heavenly spirits, who would grant their wishes.

As this 1870s engraving shows, kite flying has been a popular activity in China for many years.

Eventually, the Chinese realized the potential military uses for kites. For instance, they flew kites to call troops into action. Chinese army spies used kites in the form of eagles to fly above enemy troops to report on their deployment. One famous general sent up men in giant kites to play music on flutes in order to make enemy soldiers homesick and cause them to retreat.

In a famous Han Dynasty episode, the empire was saved through kite tactics. Enemy forces were deployed on the vulnerable side of the Emperor's palace. A Han minister ordered that kites be fitted with bamboo bows and launched in the dead of night. The bamboo bows produced eerie sounds as they vibrated in the wind. Low moans and high-pitched wails filled the night air, sending enemy soldiers into panic. Spies were sent among the enemy troops to spread rumors that they would be destroyed by the howling spirits they heard. Terrified by the noise and rumors, the enemy troops fled and the Chinese empire was saved.

Today, these military functions of kites are reflected in the sport of **kite fighting**. Ground glass or sand is applied to about 100 feet (30 meters) of glue-covered line nearest the kites. Using the lines as saws, the fliers try to cut their opponents' kites loose from their lines. The competitors fly the kites low to the ground to allow daring swoops, dodges, and quick darts that will allow them to slice through their opponents' lines. Scary monsters decorate the kites to increase the chance of victory. The victor wins both the contest and his opponent's kite.

The Chinese also have used kites as working tools for fishing and farming. Some fishermen needn't venture out onto water in a boat. By attaching bait to a string on a kite tail, Chinese fishermen could pull in their catch from the safety of the shore.

When the Chinese invented paper during the Han Dynasty (206 B.C.–A.D. 220), many people began to build kites. With the accessibility of paper, kites became a popular amusement and were integrated into Chinese folk festivals. Today, the skies over China are filled with colorful kites, which the Chinese call *feng zhen,* or "wind zither," because of the sound of the wind as it passes through holes in the bamboo frame.

China is a vast country with different climates and wind conditions. The Chinese have adapted the design of their kites to suit each special climatic condition. South of the Yangtze River, the weather is rainy and humid with mild winds. Here, the Chinese use a soft-wing type of kite. These kites have wings that flap. Kites in south-

Preparing to launch a very long dragon kite

ern China are decorated with pictures of birds, butterflies, and insects to match this soft-wing design.

North of the Yangtze River, the weather is arid and windy. Here, the Chinese use hard-winged kites. These kites have tassels or ropes trailing after them to steady them during sudden wind shifts. Bamboo bows, whistles, drums, and gongs may all be attached to the kites to add music to their flight in the brisk wind conditions.

The Chinese most often use designs of swallows on hard-winged kites. Since these birds bond for life, they are an auspicious decorative motif. Dragons are another common design in the north. In ancient days, the belief that dragons could bring rain led to the performance of dragon dances at the Lunar New Year. The Chinese paint dragons down the middle of their kites with striped clouds and watery waves on each side. This design shows the dragon leaping into the clouds and diving into the sea as the kite rises and falls.

A young girl with her hard-winged kite in Beijing, China

Bat designs also are popular for kites, since the Chinese word for "bat" is pronounced the same as the word for "blessing." Centipede kites are made by stringing a number of kites together.

Chinese folklore characters are also used to decorate kites. One popular figure is Lady Chang Er, a woman who, according to the story, stole the elixir of immortality and flew to the moon, where she became a fairy who lived in a palace. Paired butterflies are also a popular folk design on kites. Butterfly lovers represent the Romeo and Juliet story of a young couple who could not marry. They were transformed into butterflies after their deaths.

This woman makes elaborate soft-winged kites in the shapes of the dragonfly and phoenix.

# Chapter Five

# Puppets

Another handmade form of entertainment is puppets. Chinese call puppetry "theater within the palm." One Chinese saying goes: "The puppeteer tells a thousand stories with one breath and creates a dance of one million soldiers with two hands."

Archaeologists have found examples of Chinese puppets in tombs of the Zhou Dynasty (1100–221 B.C.). These were figurines made of clay and wood with movable body parts. Archaeologists theorize that these puppets took the place of real human beings who at one time were forced to follow their masters to the tomb. It is possible, archaeologists believe, that these puppets were operated by a shaman (or sorcerer) during funeral performances or exorcisms. They would persuade the soul of the dead person to enter a puppet so as to direct it safely to the underworld. Or, they would use some puppets to drive away evil influences and pestilence.

Chinese puppets called jumping jacks

From funerals, the use of puppets expanded to happy occasions, such as weddings and festivals. Accompanied by music, puppet performances became part of entertainment rather than rites and have retained that role in China for several thousand years.

By the Song Dynasty (A.D. 960–1280), a section of the capital city was designated "the pleasure quarter," an area for many different kinds of entertainment. Small puppetry troupes set up their portable stages near bridges in the pleasure quarter so as to coincide with traffic. The puppeteers rubbed elbows with street vendors, jugglers, acrobats, satirists, and comics who specialized in the telling of dirty jokes.

The porcelain head of this puppet is removable so the character can have several costume changes.

Some puppet troupes enjoyed the patronage of wealthy merchants or aristocrats — perhaps the Emperor himself. Others performed in teahouses or singing halls. They would travel into the country when small villages pooled resources to finance several days of performances during festivals. The art of puppetry was passed from father to son. Each family jealously guarded its secrets of performance and scripts.

The most popular type of puppet in China today is the hand puppet.

A cotton glove or shell forms the upper body and is controlled by the puppeteer's hand. This type of hand puppet is easily manipulated in complex gestures and movements. Hand puppeteers specialize in plays featuring martial arts and acrobatics. The puppets have removable heads so that one character may have several costume changes.

The costumes and makeup of hand puppets are very elaborate as in Chinese opera. Spectators recognize the personality of a character by the color of the makeup. Red faces denote bravery, while white faces show cunning or treachery. Puppets with black faces are known for their loyalty.

A beautiful and complex Chinese puppet theater

Elementary-school children put on a shadow puppet show. The audience, on the other side of the screen, sees only the shadows of the characters that the children are moving with sticks.

Shadow puppets are also a popular form of entertainment in China. This form of puppetry probably evolved around the time the Chinese invented paper during the Han Dynasty (206 B.C.–A.D. 220). Early shadow puppets were made of paper. Later, the puppets were fashioned of leather. The term for shadow-puppet theater is *pi-ying xi*, or "theater of leather shadows."

The shadows are actually silhouettes seen by the audience when light penetrates a sheet of translucent cloth. Since shadow puppets are two-dimensional, they are unable to exhibit changes of facial expression. Shadow puppeteers rely upon music and song to express the sentiments of the characters.

Shadow puppeteers can create many exciting special effects. Shadow puppet performances may include magical transformations, beheadings, or complicated fighting scenes. Enactments of ancient battles are especially spectacular. Puppeteers can cause a shadow figure to launch an arrow, or they can create large armies out of a few figures by shining lights behind the figures to create multiple shadows on the screen. They create sound effects of mounted warriors by striking a box to imitate horses' hooves or using Chinese oboes called *suo-na* to create the neighing of stallions.

**Marionettes** represent the oldest type of puppets found in China. These are the puppets that were traditionally used in exorcisms and rituals. Chinese weddings, birthdays, or unhappy occasions, such as fires or deaths, required a string-puppet performance to expel evil forces or appease the spirits. Because of the belief that spirits could inhabit them, Chinese marionettes were always kept locked away with their heads stored separately.

Marionette puppetry is called *tie-xian xi* (or "wire theater"). The puppets are controlled by puppeteers hidden behind long, silk curtains on either side of the stage. These puppets may be up to 3 feet (90 cm) tall, with elaborate costumes and delicately carved heads. Traditionally, heads might be carved from camphor wood and bodies made from bamboo and hemp. Today, marionettes are more likely to be made of plastic.

Strings control the marionette's head, limbs, and shoulders. Originally, there were eight strings, but today's puppets may have as many as 32 strings. Traditional silk string may now have given way to nylon, but the stories performed continue to be the tales that have entertained the Chinese for centuries.

Unlike the forceful, staccato style of hand puppets, marionettes move in graceful, synchronized choreography. Deft gestures identify each character. Backdrops and scenery are never used, and props are kept to a minimum.

The most widespread type of puppet in China is the rod puppet. The Chinese term for rod puppet is *zhang-tou mu-ou,* meaning "staff-head puppet." This refers to the construction of the puppets with a hidden central control staff operated. Smaller rods to control the hands may be concealed within the costume of the puppet.

Rod puppets are found in every province in China. They vary considerably in size and construction ranging from puppets about a foot high to life-sized puppets with movable eyes, eyelids, mouth, tongue, ears, and nose.

Chinese children are entertained by a marionette show.

# Chapter Six
# Sports in China

Balls are among the oldest toys ever unearthed by Chinese archaeologists. Balls made of both stone and pottery have been excavated at the Neolithic village of Banpo from the six-thousand-year-old Yangshao culture.

**F**ootball in China originally served as a military training exercise. Players used a ball made of softened leather stuffed with goosedown. The ball was kicked with the feet or punched with the fists. The object was to move the ball from one person to the next without letting it touch the ground.

Later, football became a popular sport and amusement. Emperors and commoners played it during the Song Dynasty. There are written accounts of Song football clubs with names like "Equal with the Clouds" and "Round Circle."

Today, **soccer**, known as "football" outside of North America, is among the most popular sports in China. In 1991, the first-ever women's world soccer championship was held in China. That game was won by the United States women's team. During the 1996 Olympics, held in Atlanta, Georgia, the American women again took the first-place gold medal, and the Chinese women's team came away with the second-place silver.

A Chinese soccer player in the 1996 Olympics

**Polo**, a sport requiring bravery and skillful horsemanship, was originally developed as a military exercise. In ancient China, Persia, India, Egypt, Greece, and Japan, the game was used to train cavalry soldiers.

Wall paintings from the Han Dynasty show Chinese nobles engaged in a fierce game of polo. The northern nomadic tribes of China doubtless developed this sport. With these tribes' absorption into Chinese society, polo became part of China's traditional games.

Today's version of polo has rules designed to make the game safer. Two competing teams use mallets with long, flexible handles to drive a wooden ball across the field. One scores by shooting the ball across the other team's goal line to earn each point. The polo field is the largest field of any ball game in the world. Each goal is 8 feet (2.4 m) wide and 10 feet (3.0 m) high.

In the Chinese game of **jianzi**, a shuttlecock is kept in the air as long as possible by catching it on the heel or sole of the foot. The shuttlecock is often made by

wrapping an old-style Chinese coin with a hole in the middle, or a simple disk of cardboard with a central hole, in a bit of rag or soft leather. Goose quills are poked through the central hole to help keep the shuttlecock in the air.

Moving the shuttlecock from the sole of the foot to the racket leading to the game of **badminton**, was an easy step for Chinese athletes. Today, badminton is a popular sport throughout Asia. In modern, exciting badminton matches, a shuttlecock can start off traveling at 200 miles (320 km) per hour!

Badminton became an Olympic sport in 1992. In the 1996 Olympics, China's women's team won the gold and bronze in doubles. The men took the silver in singles. China's mixed doubles team took the bronze medal.

The Chinese women's badminton team in Olympic play

The Chinese believe that the body must maintain a balance of *yin* and *yang* to remain healthy and achieve longevity. They have devised a number of sports and exercises that promote this balance. These traditional Chinese sports stress individual perfection rather than team effort. Artistry, form, and balance are all goals of these sports.

*Gongfu* is a term that has entered the English language largely due to the influence of **martial arts** films and the star, Bruce Lee. The term, as used today, includes martial arts of boxing, weapon wielding, and various methods of health maintenance.

The martial arts are a favorite activity in China and many other Asian countries.

The origin of all gongfu styles can be traced back to Shaolin Temple in Henan Province. The styles are roughly divided between northern and southern, and internal and external styles. External gongfu is said to exercise the tendons, bones, and skin. Internal gongfu trains spirit, *qi*, and mind.

Many forms of external gongfu are based upon the movements of animals found in nature. Tiger, panther, monkey, snake, and crane are the names of various styles of gongfu.

Balance, grace, flexibility, and strength are all elements of traditional **acrobatics**. Archaeologists have unearthed ceramic statues of acrobats balancing pottery containers on their heads that date from the Shang Dynasty (1700–1100 B.C.). Acrobatics are key acts in the Chinese circus and are featured in Chinese entertainments such as Peking opera.

Tightrope balancing; juggling swords, balls, and pottery containers; tumbling; and spinning disks and plates on bamboo or rattan poles are other types of acrobatic sports and entertainment that continue to be popular today. Some acrobatic groups from China have toured the United States and won great acclaim for their performances.

Chinese acrobats seem to defy the laws of gravity.

Chinese Olympic gymnastics champion Li Xiaoshuang in action on the high bar

Chinese athletes have built upon traditional acrobatics to produce outstanding male and female athletes in **gymnastics**. During the 1996 Olympic Games, the men's gymnastic team captured the silver medal in the team competition. Li Xiaoshuang won a gold medal for individual all-around competition and a silver for floor exercise. Fan Bi took the bronze for high bar.

Mo Huilan of the women's team won a silver for vault and Bi Wenjing won a bronze on uneven bars. Amy Chow, a Chinese-American from San Jose, California, took the silver for uneven bars.

Displaying the same superb combination of balance, grace, and athleticism as the gymnastics team, the Chinese men's and women's **diving** teams swept the field in Atlanta. In springboard diving, Fu Mingxia won the women's gold, Xiong Na the men's gold, and Yu Zhuocheng the men's silver. Chinese divers were also strong in platform diving, taking the women's gold, and the bronze medal for the men.

In the water, Chinese women excelled in **swimming**. The team took six Olympic medals. Swimmer Le Jingyi won the gold in the 100-meter freestyle and the silver in the 50-meter freestyle.

Fu Mingxia, a diver on the Chinese women's team at the 1996 Olympics

Ping-Pong was not invented in China, but Chinese kids love to play!

Contrary to popular belief, **Ping-Pong** is not a Chinese invention. A London toyshop owner, Walter Hamley, introduced the game in 1910. He named it "Table Tennis," or "Gossamer." Nevertheless, Ping-Pong is widespread throughout Asia today, and Chinese children are avid enthusiasts.

In 1974, America normalized relations with Beijing by sending a team of American Ping-Pong players to compete in China. The

Americans lost every game, but laid the foundations for a new political era.

In 1996, the Chinese table tennis team competing at the Olympics in Atlanta swept the field. The women's singles won gold, silver, and bronze medals for China's team. Athletes from The People's Republic of China took the gold and bronze. Chen Jing of Taiwan, Republic of China, took the silver. Gold and silver medals were won by the women's team in doubles. In men's singles, Chinese athletes took the gold and silver, and the gold and silver in men's doubles.

Table tennis in the 1996 Olympics

# Glossary

**agrarian society**
A civilization based upon a farming way of life — traditional Chinese life is based on the harvesting of rice, millet, and wheat

**archaeology**
The scientific study of material remains of past human life and activities

**diabolo**
barbell-shaped hollow spinning toy that hums as it is manipulated on a string

**dragon**
mythical beast with body parts of many other animals; unlike the Western dragon, which eats princesses and destroys crops, the Chinese dragon helps farmers by bringing rain

**dynasty**
a succession of rulers of the same line of descent; China's last dynasty was the Qing dynasty from 1912 to 1949

**Festival of Spring Brightness**
spring holiday when the family visits and tends the family tombs; also known as the Tomb Sweeping Festival

*go*
Japanese name for Chinese game of *weiqi*

*gongfu*
term used to refer to martial arts and sports designed for health maintenance

*jianzi*
game involving a shuttlecock that is kept aloft by catching it on the heel or sole of the foot

**Lantern Festival**
festival celebrated on the 15th day of the Lunar New Year; signals the end of the holiday season

**Lunar New Year**
the beginning of the Chinese year; usually celebrated in February

**macramé**
intricate knots used as decoration or to make decorative items

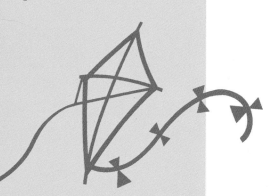

**majiang**
Chinese word for "sparrow"; also a Chinese game similar to dominoes that that uses tiles

**paper cuts**
decorations for holidays and celebrations made from colored paper

**pleasure quarter**
area of ancient Chinese cities reserved for amusements such as puppet shows and acrobats

*qi*
Chinese term meaning "dynamic energy"

*sanjiao*
Chinese word for triangle; POGS were originally folded paper triangles

*Suo-na*
Chinese oboe used for sound effects such as the neighing of horses in puppet performances

**tangram**
square divided into seven pieces that can be arranged to form different objects and shapes

*Weiqi*
China's most ancient board game; also known by its Japanese name — "go"

**yin and yang**
the two elements of the universe; yin corresponds with the female and yang with the male

*zi*
pieces used in the game of *weiqi,* or *go*

# **F**or Further Information

## Books

Falkener, Edward. **Games Ancient and Oriental and How to Play Them**. Dover Publications, 1961.

Ha, Kuiming and Yiqi Ha. **Chinese Artistic Kites**. China Books & Periodicals, Inc., 1990.

Kalman, Bobbie. **China: The Culture**. Crabtree, 1989.

Lau, H. T. **Chinese Chess**. Charles E. Tuttle Company, 1985.

McLeningham, Valjean. **People's Republic of China**. Childrens Press, 1994.

Wang, Hongxun. **Chinese Kites**. Foreign Languages Press, 1989.

Whitney, Eleanor Noss. **A Mah Jong Handbook: How to Play, Score and Win the Modern Game**. Charles E. Tuttle Company, 1993.

## Online Sites

**Cathay Arts**
http://www.maui.net/~cthyarts/cathay_arts_home.html
Online site for an art gallery that specializes in contemporary Chinese arts and crafts.

**China Monthly**
http://www.chinamz.org/
An online magazine with information about Chinese culture and politics.

**Chinese Culture Online**
http://www.brainlink.com/~kkin/ccol.html
Illustrations, art, and lots of information about Chinese culture—past and present.

**Chinese New Year**
http://dae.com/cny/
Celebrate Chinese New Year online with thousands of people from around the world.

**Chinese Olympic Team**
http://olympics.asianews.com/
Full coverage of how the Chinese team performed at the 1996 Summer Olympics.

# Index

(**Boldface** page numbers indicate illustrations.)

## Photo Credits

## About the Author
Kim Dramer is a Ph.D. candidate in the Department of Art History & Archaeology at Columbia University. Her books for young adults have ranged from a biography of Kublai Khan to Indians of North America. She is the mother of twins, Alex and Max (Wang Xian Tang and Wang Xian Han), who enjoy many of the toys and customs described in this book.